Catho

Experiencing

Catholics Experiencing Divorce

Grieving, Healing, and Learning to Live Again

Revised Edition

VICKI WELLS BEDARD
AND WILLIAM E. RABIOR

Liguori

LIGUORI, MISSOURI

Imprimi Potest: Richard Thibodeau, C.Ss.R.,
Provincial, Denver Province, The Redemptorists

Imprimatur: Most Reverend Robert J. Hermann
Auxiliary Bishop of St. Louis

Published by Liguori Publications, Liguori, Missouri
www.liguori.org

Library of Congress Cataloging-in-Publication Data

Bedard, Vicki Wells.
    Catholics experiencing divorce / grieving, healing, and learning to live again.—
Rev. ed. / Vicki Wells Bedard and William E. Rabior.
        p. cm.
    Rev. ed. of: Catholics experiencing divorce / William E. Rabior and Vicki Wells Bedard.
        ISBN 0-7648-1157-6 (pbk.)
    1. Divorce—Religious aspects—Catholic Church. 2. Divorced people—Religious life. I. Rabior, William E. II. Bedard, Vicki Wells. Catholics experiencing divorce. III. Title.

BX2254.R33 2004
248.8'46—dc22   2003069492

Scripture citations are taken from the *New Revised Standard Version of the Bible*, copyright 1989 by the Division of Christian Education of the National Council of the Churches of Christ in the USA. All rights reserved. Used with permission.

Printed in the United States of America
08 07 06 05 04   5 4 3 2 1
Revised edition 2004

Contents

Introduction vii

CHAPTER ONE: FROM COUPLENESS TO SINGLENESS 1

The Role of Church and Community 3
Losing the Safety Net of Marriage 7
Become Your Own Best Friend 8

CHAPTER TWO: FROM LOSS TO ACCEPTANCE 17

The Stages of Grief 19
The Aim of Good Grieving 22
Grieving and Prayer 24
The Quest for Intimacy 24

CHAPTER THREE: FROM PAIN TO PEACE 31

You and God 33
You and the Church 35
You and the Community 38
You and Your Own Resources 43

CHAPTER FOUR: FROM DARKNESS TO NEW LIFE 45

One Day at a Time 46
Starting Over 47
Do What You Love… 50
God and Your Future 51
Remarriage 51

Conclusion 61

APPENDIX 1: USING THE INTERNET WISELY AND WELL 63

APPENDIX 2: SUGGESTIONS FOR RELIABLE RESOURCES 67

Introduction

How do you describe divorce? What does it look like, sound like, feel like? What does it do to and for the persons who experience it?

Perhaps the most appropriate response to these multiple questions may be a story—the old tale of the blindfolded men who were asked to describe an elephant based exclusively on their sense of touch. Each man's description reflected what he touched and perceived in that touch. The man who felt the trunk based his description of the elephant on what the trunk felt like; the man who felt an ear described an elephant according to what the ear felt like; the man who felt the tail based his description on what the tail felt like. The experience of the same reality was different for each person.

That is exactly the case for Brian, Mary Ann, Allen, and Suzanne. Each has experienced a divorce, and each has a very different perception of that experience.

Brian: "For me, divorce was unquestionably the most painful event of my entire life. It was worse than the death of a loved one because death has a certain finality to it. Divorce doesn't. It's been eight years now, and I still find myself angry at what happened. I am very aware that the bickering between my former wife and myself is a manifestation of the fact that I still haven't fully healed from the experience."

Mary Ann: "I'd have to say that for the most part divorce was a good thing for me. It opened doors to a better and happier life for my children and myself. My marriage was a disaster. I was living in an abusive situation with an alcoholic husband who wouldn't seek any kind of help for himself and who took out his illness every day on the kids and me. It was nightmarish at best.

"After trying many things that did not work, I finally realized that divorce was the only option left—the only way I could salvage my sanity and stop the pain my children and I were living in. And that's exactly what it turned out to be—a passageway to a safe haven. To this day, I believe it was God's will for me to leave that marriage rather than be destroyed. I would do it again for the same reasons."

Allen: "I believe I got a divorce too quickly and too easily. Our state has a no-fault divorce law, so we were able to end a seven-year marriage in less than four months. Now I really wish we had worked harder to save it. It's been nearly two years since my divorce, and I'd have to say that I still grieve the loss of my marriage."

Suzanne: "I married a man who was opposed to having children. The tragedy was that I didn't find that out until after we were married. I was a victim of his lies. I obtained both a divorce as well as a Church annulment and have happily remarried. I also have a beautiful baby daughter from my second marriage. So for me, divorce was the only way out of a deception that I simply could not live with."

Four persons—four very different experiences of divorce. There is no such thing as a garden-variety, or "typical," divorce. Circumstances may look typical, but each divorce scenario is colored and shaped by the unique persons and events involved. Divorce is a complicated response to complex marital problems.

We know that divorce is an increasingly common phenomenon. Current statistics suggest that as many as one out of every two marriages will end in a divorce. More recent research also indicates that the emotional fallout from a divorce can persist much longer than originally anticipated. Anger, resentment, and other very strong negative feelings can linger for many years and remain powerful and potent. Precisely because it tends to be such a turbulent and tumultuous event in the lives of most persons, time alone does not heal all the wounds associated with a divorce.

This book is not meant to be a cure-all for the many thorny problems linked to divorce. Nor is it presented as some kind of ultimate self-help manual. On the contrary, its goals are far more modest.

The following reflections and suggestions are meant to underscore and highlight approaches to coping with a divorce from a Catholic perspective—approaches that have proved helpful to many others who have passed the same way.

This book is solution-oriented, not problem-oriented. The major theme that unifies this book is that divorce generally requires some degree of emotional and spiritual healing. We fully recognize that for each individual who has experienced a divorce, the level of hurt or woundedness and the corresponding need for healing will be different and unique to his or her circumstances.

We offer this book as our contribution to the facilitation of a genuine healing process in your life. In some small way, may it assist you in opening doors to a happier, healthier, and more hope-filled life following your experience of divorce.

Chapter One

From Coupleness
to Singleness

T hat is why a man leaves his father and mother and clings to his wife, and the two of them become one body." This reading commonly used at wedding ceremonies comes from Genesis 2:4. But exactly what is a couple? A couple is a unit of two persons.

Class reunions offer "couple" tickets for a cheaper price than two single tickets. Motel accommodations are cheaper for two people if they get a "double" room rather than two "singles." Châteaubriand is on the menu for two.

Following your divorce you suddenly are no longer a twosome; you're a "onesome." In a world that endorses the theory that "two can live as cheaply as one," how high is the price you must now pay for your singleness?

Sherrie, a divorce veteran of two years, answers the question this way: "Expensive? Let me tell you about it. Everything that required maintenance expired within two months after my divorce. The fridge and television died, the car shook and rattled—you name it. Just going 'into the valley' wasn't enough emotionally. Oh, no, I had to take the long journey into credit bureaus as well."

Sherrie isn't alone when she interprets "expense" in terms of dollar signs. One couple going through an amicable divorce said there ought to be a shower for the soon-to-be-divorced:"We spent twelve months preparing and saving for the expense of our wedding, which came to about six thousand dollars. With lawyer and broker fees and moving costs, we've reached that amount in just three months since our decision to separate. It doesn't take long to use up whatever you've accumulated over the years.

In more hostile divorces, court costs alone can exceed all joint assets, leaving the couple with a newly acquired debt and deep bitterness as their only settlement.

Some marriage counselors suggest that an enforced waiting period, legal and marital counseling, and some discussion of the disposition and sharing of material goods should take place before a wedding. "If the wedding costs were equal to court costs and legal fees for divorcing, maybe marriages would be entered into with more serious thought," said one counselor who works for Catholic Charities. "The Church, too, needs to heed the voices of those who have been through a divorce, voices insisting that preparation for marriage is the best preventive medicine."

Divorce is expensive on all levels—emotionally, spiritually, socially, and financially. Consequently, divorce is physically expensive as well.

More reality—two *do not* live as cheaply as one. Two share the basic expenses that are approximately the same whether single or married.

"I had two choices," observes Sherrie. "Either get rid of a lot of stuff and move to something smaller and less expensive or get another job to keep the same standard of living."

Experts tend to agree with Sherrie. Studies find that while a man's standard of living may actually increase after a divorce by as much as 50 percent, a woman's standard of living may decline by as much as 73 percent. The average woman is likely to earn only about two-thirds of what her male peer makes in the same field. At the same time, it is usually the woman who retains physical custody of the children, which in many instances compounds her financial problems.

The Role of Church and Community

Where do you turn for help following a divorce? Many people want to turn to the Church but are often disappointed by the response they receive. "If I thought the Church had little to offer me when I was a young married person, I had a lot more to learn about what is not available to single, divorced people," laments Bernice, a newly divorced Catholic. This view is frequently expressed by Catholics who have entered the single state following their divorce.

If society is couple-oriented, then we can expect that the Church who views the family as its basic building block will follow the same pattern. While society, however, has removed much of the stigma attached to divorce, the Church has not moved as rapidly in that direction.

Lynn, now in her forties, recalls a traumatic experience with her church community ten years ago when she was going through a divorce: "John and I were part of a prayer group at church. When we separated, I asked the group for prayers. I was shocked into tears at the 'prayers' we received: 'Lord, show them the error of their ways…bring them out of their selfishness…forgive their sins against you and the institution of marriage.'

"I could hardly believe my ears! John and I came to this decision slowly and carefully. We used professional counselors and grieved a lot over our decision. We were two people hurting

3

badly, and we needed loving support. We didn't need to be scolded or scalded with guilt for giving up or throwing away a gift from God."

What Lynn and John learned is shared by many other separated and divorced couples: a failed marriage often is seen as a threat that will weaken all marriages. If a "good Christian marriage" doesn't survive, what does that mean for both the believing community as well as the rest of society?

We do not get married in a vacuum. Marriages are community events. Parents, brothers and sisters, aunts and uncles, grandparents—the entire family plus friends, business acquaintances, and even old flames—are all invited to witness the union of two people. The couple's pledge is echoed throughout the community—a community being renewed by the couple's love and desire to build a new life and family together.

So much about the beginning of a marriage is shared by the community. Detailed marriage announcements fill the newspapers, invitation designers thrive, reception arrangements are made in anticipation of offering adequate hospitality, and during the ceremony itself, the gathered assembly is asked to extend some sign of affirmation and blessing toward the two who are bonding their lives. Everyone everywhere shares in the wonder of the couple's joy when they get married.

However, when it comes to divorce, there is absolutely nothing—no ceremony, no church acknowledgment, no outpouring of community support. In cities where the newspapers print a list of divorce decrees, the announcements are quietly buried on a back page.

As a society and a Church, we are ill-prepared to cope with the uncoupling process. There are no rites or traditions that take over and carry us through. And Miss Manners can't supply us with the proper etiquette to make things easy, simple, and tasteful.

Lynn continues: "About six months after our divorce, an acquaintance of ours lost his wife to cancer. At the funeral luncheon I was shaken by the mix of emotions flooding through me. I grieved with him and his family at the seemingly pointless loss and the ending of so much.

"And then I looked around and saw the outpouring of love and affection he was getting from people. They held him and cried with him. Nobody blamed him or his wife. No one said she was at fault because she smoked two packs of cigarettes a day. No one criticized him because the stress of his career made her nervous and drove her to smoke. People just wanted to be supportive.

"I am ashamed to admit it, but suddenly that made me jealous. Not one of the persons I knew from church or school functions had asked me how I was doing or if the children and I needed anything.

"It was as if I had gone through something enormously embarrassing by getting a divorce. The widowed could be objects of compassion, but I could not be. It took me a long time to work things through, and I still get somewhat rankled at the 'outcast' I once was."

Lynn's remarks are very perceptive. Divorce and separation tend to create an embarrassing situation for both the couple and the society in which they live. If people are at a loss for words at the death of a family member, what do they say to someone who decides to "untie" the knot of matrimony?

Many times the uncomfortableness comes from the couple themselves as they sort out all their feelings and memories. One or both may feel they have failed. If one is labeled the "good guy," the other may well become the "bad guy." Friendships and family loyalties often become stressed with the burden of "choosing sides." This makes an already uncomfortable situation that much more painful.

We don't get married to get divorced. We get married because we believe our lives will be intimately more satisfying if shared with another rather than experiencing life without a partner. Sometimes, and for many different reasons, our dreams don't come true. Sometimes we simply and humbly have to admit that we made a mistake.

When we make that admission, others are forced to look at their own commitments. Just as a wedding will cause married couples to reflect on their own wedding day and experience affirmation in the choice they made, divorce causes the same couples to question the wisdom of their choice: "Could this happen to us?" This can make some persons feel vulnerable and uneasy. For those especially uncomfortable in their own situation, divorce causes resentment: "If I can live in a lousy marriage for forty years, what gives them the right to give up after five?"

"Divorcing forced John and me to dialogue," Lynn says. "For the first time in years, we had nothing to lose by saying it all. At first, we thought that opening the lines of communication would bring us together. But we soon found that our differences were too great. We had grown too far apart.

"Our marriage had become dysfunctional; it had ceased being a source of love, fulfillment, and growth. For us, divorce was the best decision."

Merely being confronted with the reality of divorce can be exceedingly painful for marriages that survive by keeping unpleasant things locked away. Association with those who have faced their problems and have chosen to leave a marriage is often far too threatening.

In general, transitions tend to be highly anxiety producing. Divorce is no exception; in fact, it ranks as one of the top three major stressors in life.

Elaine, now in her fifties, married when she was eighteen. She explains how her transition to oneness was overwhelming. "Eating alone in restaurants became the most depressing experience I had ever known. Have you ever noticed people buried under newspapers trying to look like they don't mind that no one is there to talk to them?

"I would always try to avoid looking up. I didn't want the other diners to think, 'Aw, poor lady. No one to eat with her.' I just knew that's what they were thinking because I had thought the very same thing ever since I was a child."

Losing the Safety Net of Marriage

It could be argued that it doesn't matter whether marriages are good or bad because there is a certain safety in the magical number two. Jason, divorced three years, explains some of the benefits his marriage afforded him. "Married to Bonnie, I automatically had the convenience of a built-in date. I could flirt, look around, meet other women, and I was 'safe.' If I smiled at a woman across the room and she frowned, I'd find myself running over to Bonnie, throwing the woman an 'I don't care, I don't need you anyway' look.

"I know a lot of other married men who are grateful that they don't have to handle the social pressure of entertaining the opposite sex. One dance with the wife and you can get back to table talk. If flirting gets out of hand, you can always flash your 'married' look and be safe."

Even if a marriage is coming to an end, a safety net may still exist—a safety net that may serve as a network for future social contacts. Oftentimes, prospects for important social encounters are lined up before the divorce decree is signed. For example, Theresa used her pending divorce as a conversation opener: "I would explain that I was going through a rough time with the divorce. Suddenly, I would have an audience of interested gentlemen, many saying they had gone through the same thing. This was the foundation for future conversations. The safety part came from the fact that I wasn't yet divorced, so when the direction would look like it was going to shift from talking and move toward more active participation, I could simply beg off."

Theresa and Jason are not unique examples. It appears that most of what life deals out is handled more easily by a couple—even a couple who no longer function well together.

The cliché, "The devil you know is better than the devil you don't know," sums up the reason so many dysfunctional marriages, even dead ones, limp onward. Fear of the alternatives can be enough to keep people together for a lifetime, even if they are tragically unhappy.

In any event, you have decided to become "one" again. You recognize that it is a costly decision on many levels, including the personal level. What can you do for yourself?

Become Your Own Best Friend

"I knew I had to find a group to support me," Lynn recalls. "I checked with our local Catholic Charities office and found there were several groups for the separated and divorced within driving distance.

"So I literally shopped around until I found one I was comfortable with. I especially wanted one that was positive and provided a safe haven for me. I really came to love the people in that group. We not only shared our feelings but also covered practical things like preparing tax forms, car maintenance, and insurance needs. I taught one fellow how to cook spaghetti and he showed me how to put up storm windows."

Group involvement may not be your style; look around. You're not the only one who has ever returned to singleness. Others have gone through it before you. Seek them out.

Becoming a single person very likely has made you acutely aware of how many others share with you this same state of life. Some have never married, some are widowed. Stretch yourself, take some chances, and reach out to others. Rediscover and rekindle old relationships that you may have set aside during your years of marriage.

Primarily, learn from the pain you've experienced. You can be the one who reaches out to others going through the same rough times you've gone through. Talk to your pastor. Help him minister to those who feel isolated and wounded. Involve yourself and try to make a difference in the lives of others.

As much as you possibly can, emphasize the positive. A double bed can be terrific for one person. You don't like asparagus, so don't cook it. Want to let the dishes go until tomorrow? That's fine. Hate ribbons, bows, and flowers? Get rid of them.

You've spent a large portion of your life attempting to form yourself into a spouse/person. Now it's time to discover your self/person. The best friend you can make is yourself. Treat yourself kindly and well. Learn to see yourself the way God sees you: "You are precious in my sight, / and honored, and I love you" (Isaiah 43:4).

As you experience more dimensions of your singleness, begin to develop a fresh identity. The writer of Ecclesiastes points out that in the life cycle of human beings, there is a time to seek and a time to lose. The statement seems especially apropos when applied to divorce. For example, invariably there is some loss or alteration of your identity as a result of a divorce.

For a period of time—sometimes for several decades—your identity has been inextricably linked to that of another human being, your former spouse. Perhaps you even shared the same last name. For both men and women, there is likely to be some kind of adjustment phase related to the issue of identity.

Rachel shares some of her struggles. "Bob and I were married twenty years. I didn't want a divorce. He's the one who filed, and that plunged me into the deepest crisis of my entire life. And it affected every aspect of my life, including my identity.

"I had been Bob's wife for twenty years. Then suddenly, I was nobody's wife. In fact, I was quite alone, since the kids were pretty much grown and gone from home.

"Rebounding from the divorce was very difficult. For a time, I didn't know who or what I was. I believed that I didn't have or couldn't have a true identity without being married. My confusion became so great that I got severely depressed and even thought of suicide."

Rachel sighs, then smiles, "Thank God for my doctor! He directed me to a counselor who specialized in helping women create a new life following a divorce. With her help, I began to see that married or unmarried I am a good person with dignity and a lot of worth.

"My thinking had become so distorted and irrational that it was destroying me. With counseling, I learned how to see and interpret things differently. Thanks to the help I received I'm much more comfortable now with who and what I am—a single parent with no thought of remarrying at the present time."

Coming out of the experience of divorce, a person almost always finds herself or himself wrestling with three significant questions: Who was I? Who am I? Who will I be? A complete response to these questions requires the passage of time, as well as some distancing from the divorce itself. If your divorce is recent, you may not yet have access to the kind of feedback and information that will help you fully understand yourself.

The following are some important considerations to keep in mind as you begin to forge a new sense of identity following your divorce.

You are more than any one role you fulfill in life. Married or single—male or female—you are a valuable, worthwhile person. Your value as a human being does not depend on your marital status.

Roles are forever changing. In fact, many more role changes are likely to be in store for you, as they are for everyone. As you come to grips with your identity, the place to start is with your personhood, not the roles you've played. Therapists commonly report that persons coming into counseling following a divorce usually identify their primary struggle with being uncertain about who they are.

You are not alone when it comes to the feelings you're experiencing. To some extent they are universal and even normal under the circumstances.

Understand yourself. Learn to like and love the person you are. You may have to get to know yourself all over again—or perhaps for the first time. If you build your new identity on the foundation of an authentic understanding and appreciation of who you are as a person, that identity is much more likely to carry you through the worst crises life can bring. Build or rebuild your identity to last a lifetime.

Don't be afraid of fear. Taking a thorough, honest look at yourself and forging a new identity can be extremely frightening. Many divorced persons refuse to do this because they're afraid of what they'll see. Unless you have the courage to face yourself and your life's circumstances, however, the formation of your authentic identity will be forever put off. Your struggle will actually become more difficult, since you will not know who and what you are as a person.

"For most of my life, I was afraid to face myself," confesses Joyce reflectively. "And the way I coped with not being honest with myself was to eat. I ate recklessly and compulsively, and it was one of the main reasons my marriage failed.

"I know now that facing the truth is infinitely better than living in fear. You know how I learned that? Through Overeaters Anonymous.

"My life was spinning out of control so fast that I knew I had nothing left to lose. So I started attending OA meetings. Using a twelve-step program, they taught me a new way to live.

"Thanks to OA, I now believe with all my heart that God loves me just the way I am—even vastly overweight. And I'm learning to love myself the way I am, while slowly working toward changing my life for the better."

Don't be afraid to do the work of rediscovering or rebuilding your identity. The payoffs will last for the rest of your life.

Befriend yourself. The old saying that often we're our own worst enemy is absolutely true. With practice and patience, we can learn to become a true and faithful friend to ourselves.

Befriending yourself is all the more crucial while rebuilding your identity. More than ever you need to be self-affirming, gentle, and kind with yourself, and appreciative of who you are.

Try harder to be less self-critical. Work at reducing those negative assessments of yourself that are harsh and merciless— assessments we too often tend to believe and accept.

One final rule of thumb in this area: treat yourself the way you would a dear old friend who has just come back into your life to stay.

Give yourself plenty of time. There is no way to rush the process of healing your wounded identity or working toward a new sense of identity.

See yourself as being in process, moving slowly and gradually toward your goal. Don't become impatient or lose heart if you don't seem to make much progress. In the area of identity, progress usually is measured not by miles but by a fraction of an inch as you discover new things about yourself. Be patient with yourself. Both God and you aren't finished with you yet.

Draw upon every resource available to you. You cannot shape a new identity, or even integrate an old and a new one, within a vacuum. You are living in a real world, and fortunately, that world has many valuable resources to offer you. These resources may include professional counseling, which provides an excellent means to address many of your identity issues. In addition, many self-help groups can provide valuable assistance.

These groups include the better-known ones such as Al-Anon and Adult Children of Alcoholics (ACOA). There are also groups that deal with codependency, relationship addiction, and many other important issues. Find out what is available in your community and consider attending a self-help group if it addresses a major need in your life.

Since our identities are so integrally linked to our families, some therapists recommend that we have as much knowledge of our family history as possible. Consider acquiring background information about your family members. In carrying out this kind of project, a person may discover that certain traits run in his or her family—and such discoveries cast considerable light on one's own behavior.

Expect pain. "No pain, no gain" seems particularly true when it comes to the issue of identity. Therapists often warn their clients of how painful the process of introspection can be. Many clients who want an easy route to self-awareness actually bolt from therapy when they discover how demanding the inner journey is. Here is part of Rob's story.

"Not just after but even during my divorce, I dated heavily, but it turned into a hollow experience. So I decided to work on myself rather than continuing to run from myself as I had been doing.

"I knew that when I stopped dating I would become very lonely, but I also decided that getting to know me was worth it. I started to do things like stay home alone on Saturday nights and listen to music or read my favorite books that had been collecting dust for years. I went for walks alone and even spent a week camping alone.

"To be honest, there were times when the loneliness was almost unbearable. Then, after a while, I started to get more comfortable with myself. I discovered that I wasn't such bad company after all and that living with myself was something I could do quite well."

Rob chuckles. "What's happening to me now? I'm doing some dating but nothing frantic or compulsive anymore. Now that I'm not afraid to be alone with myself, I take my time."

Let God help you form or re-form your identity. Thomas Merton used to say that because God is the creator of our identity, we never discover it fully until we discover God.

God has a major investment in you. Through the great prophet Isaiah, God tells us just how much we are loved: "I have called you by name, you are mine…. / You are precious in my sight, / and honored, and I love you" (43:1,4).

Our fundamental identity lies in our relationship with God. We remain forever God's beloved sons and daughters—the children of God. If our identity has been wounded or damaged, we can ask God to help us in the healing process. Prayer can also open the door to avenues of self-awareness and self-discovery that may not have been accessible had we not prayed. Meditation, Scripture reading, and listening to Christian tapes are all good ways to enrich our spiritual life and gain important insights into who we are.

A closer relationship with God will draw us nearer our true identity. God will reveal to us things about ourselves that we would otherwise never know. That is why the key to genuine self-discovery lies in deepening our walk with our Creator.

Dealing with identity issues can be a truly formidable task, yet it can also be one of the most rewarding adventures of our entire life. As we come to know who we are, we get a better sense of where we want to be. Creating a sound identity is like fashioning a good rudder that will steer us faithfully through even the most turbulent waters toward the fulfillment of our unique personal destiny.

Chapter Two

From Loss
To Acceptance

For many persons the end of a marital relationship through divorce constitutes one of the most significant of all losses in life. Consequently, grieving is a normal response and is to be expected. Anytime we lose something or someone of significance, we grieve. It is a universal experience.

Yet grieving is a unique process. It takes place at our own pace and in our own way. For some, it is over fairly quickly. For others, the grief may persist for months, even years. That was Marcia's experience.

"My husband left me for another woman. It was that simple and that excruciatingly painful. The divorce ripped me apart. In fact, for a while I thought I would lose my mind. My family feared I might become suicidal.

"I was never actively suicidal, but it did seem as though something inside of me died. There were many, many days when I had a difficult time functioning. Looking back I can see I was depressed in a major way.

"It probably took me at least two years to grieve my divorce. I know that's a long time, but I couldn't seem to help myself. When you're hurting as badly as I was, you just can't will it away or wish it away. The hurt worked itself out at its own pace, and eventually I started to appreciate life again. I knew then I was on my way toward healing."

Does Marcia have any advice for those experiencing similar emotional pain stemming from a divorce?

"If I had it to do over, I would seek help immediately. I was in the grips of some heavy-duty grieving with lots and lots of depression. My mistake was trying to fight my way out of it by myself.

"I now wish I had talked to a professional trained in grief counseling. With some competent help, I might have worked things through more quickly. My advice? Don't grieve by yourself. Find someone to help you. It's just too hard to handle alone."

Grieving is a highly complicated response to the feeling of loss. It can have strong emotional and physical aspects to it. A person who is grieving, for example, may experience a whole range of somatic complaints, such as headaches, appetite and weight loss, insomnia, and very real sensations of physical pain.

The grief that comes from a divorce can have a spiritual component as well. "I have been through two traumatic divorces," Liz quietly admits. "Both my husbands were alcoholics. After the second failure, I thought that somehow God was punishing me. I know now that my thinking was irrational. At the time, though, it seemed awfully real to me.

"I grew frightened and more and more anxious. I even began to think I was condemned to hell and that affected my ability to function normally. For instance, I would find myself driving my car at very slow speeds so I wouldn't get into an accident and have to stand before God.

"Finally, in my desperation, I went to see my pastor who is an excellent counselor. He showed me how distorted and confused my thinking had become. He helped me to see that I was attracted to men who reminded me of my alcoholic father—men I wanted to 'fix,' just as I always wanted to fix my dad's drinking problem.

"With my pastor's help, I made peace with God and myself. It's amazing how your emotions—especially fear—can sometimes seize control of your life and take you on a terrible roller-coaster ride that leaves you dizzy and disturbed. Thank God, I was able to get off that roller coaster."

Grief is our attempt to purge the pain of loss. For the most part, it is perfectly normal and natural. Yet, as Liz indicates, grieving can become seriously impaired and render our lives dysfunctional. Working through grief in a healthy way constitutes a major goal for those who have experienced the loss of a marriage through divorce.

The Stages of Grief

Dr. Elisabeth Kubler-Ross, who pioneered much of the early research related to grieving, describes the five stages or responses of grief—denial, anger, bargaining, depression, and acceptance. Some persons pass through these stages rapidly. Others bog down or fixate in one of the stages for a long time. That's what happened to Todd.

"I'd taken several psychology courses and knew all about the stages of grieving. So when I went through my divorce, I was aware of what was happening to me, but I seemed powerless to stop any of it. I took a nosedive into the anger stage and didn't want to come out. I stayed mad for years—mad at my former wife and mad at myself."

Todd sees how getting bogged down in one stage of grieving causes tremendous pain to all involved. "What a colossal waste of time and energy. Unfortunately, to make things worse, I used my kids as part of my anger strategies. Because I didn't want any contact with their mother, I stopped seeing them. Naturally, they felt crushed. Everyone got hurt, most of all me.

"I found out that anger was a luxury I just couldn't afford. I was being held prisoner by my anger and finally knew I had to stop it or I'd lose much more than just my marriage. I would lose myself and my integrity as a person and as a parent. I ceased being angry when I accepted the fact that the price for my anger was just too high to pay."

Grief does not always listen to reason. It isn't unusual to find a grieving person ignoring certain aspects of reality, because reality is just too difficult to face. For example, just because a marriage has ended in the courts does not mean it has ended emotionally. Carol continued to feel married for a long time after the court ruled her marriage dissolved. "Duane and I had gone together since high school and were married twenty years when we divorced. Apart from my father, he was the only man I ever loved. He was the only man I ever dated.

"We had a troubled marriage and neither of us was happy. Yet when he told me he was filing for divorce, I went into shock. I just could not accept the fact that he was leaving me.

"Even after the judge pronounced our marriage over, I didn't feel divorced. I wore my wedding ring for the next five years because I still felt married. One day a male coworker at my office, a very fine man and a widower, asked me if I would consider dating him. I was horrified and told him absolutely not. When he pressed me for a reason, I made up some lame excuse and hurried away."

What helped change Carol's attitudes?

"I made a Beginning Experience Weekend offered through my parish. It helps people work through major life changes and focus on healing and self-renewal. On that weekend, I finally faced reality. I knew my marriage was over and nothing would ever change that fact. The week after, I saw my pastor and started proceedings for a Church annulment which was finally granted."

Carol laughs. "God is full of surprises. That widower at the office never gave up on me. Last year at Christmastime we were married. I am happy again, and it's wonderful!"

The grieving that tends to accompany divorce is directly impacted by one's sense of self-worth. Persons with high self-esteem do better following a divorce. They are less devastated and make necessary adjustments more quickly.

On the other hand, persons with low self-esteem who possess little psychological autonomy have a much more difficult time coping and adjusting. They do not have the ability to stand on their own two feet and experience themselves as having value independent of their spouse. It takes these persons longer to process the grief related to their divorce.

Grief research also suggests that women and men tend to grieve differently. Women are much more likely to draw upon their social support systems, such as close friends, to assist them through the grieving process.

Men, on the other hand, are apt to keep their grief to themselves—bottling it up, suppressing it, or denying it completely. As a result, men are more vulnerable to depression, which is usually a major component of the grieving process.

Dale's story is not unusual. "I bottled up my feelings following my divorce and turned to the bottle. I began to drink heavily to deaden the emotional pain inside. But it was a no-win situation because the booze only made me feel worse."

What turned things around for Dale?

"My kids saw that I was going down the tubes, so they did something called an 'intervention.' They invited some family members, a few close friends, and even my boss to my home one night to confront me about my drinking problem.

"They all laid their cards on the table. The group was loving, but very firm. They pointed out that I was destroying myself, but that it wasn't too late to heal. My boss even made arrangements for me to take time off from work so I could get inpatient treatment. The recovery process forced me to take an honest look at my divorce and how I had contributed to the failure of the marriage.

"I'm feeling a thousand percent better about myself now. I go regularly to Alcoholics Anonymous meetings and appreciate life like I never did before. Miracles still happen. God as my Higher Power saved me, and I'm going to let him keep saving me so I can have a better and better life."

The Aim of Good Grieving

The aim of grief work is not to erase painful memories associated with divorce so we become amnesiacs. Rather, good grieving makes those memories less haunting and controlling. Good grieving frees us from the mire of strong feelings so we can once again say yes to life.

Grief work is seldom a once-and-for-all event. It tends to be repetitive. Most likely we will feel the need to express our grief over and over until it is finally gone.

The grief stemming from a divorce can be overwhelming and agonizingly painful. Because of this, the temptation may be to ignore it and hope it will go away. It may—or it may not.

Ignoring grief can actually be dangerous to our physical, emotional, and spiritual well-being. Unresolved grief can take a terrible toll on our peace of mind. For long periods of time, it can affect us in ways we may not fully realize.

How, then, does a person grieving from a divorce come to some level of acceptance and peace? Instead of trying to do the grief work alone, talk through your grief with someone you trust. Your attempts to resolve and dissipate the grief will be far more effective if you seek the help of others.

Most clergy are trained in grief counseling. Therapists are also available through Catholic Charities or your local community mental-health agency. Both are usually listed under "Mental Health Services" in the Yellow Pages of your telephone directory.

In many communities, there are support groups that specifically focus on the grief, pain, and adjustments associated with divorce. To find such a group, check the public-service announcements in your local newspaper. Remember: asking for help is a sign of courage, not weakness. It means you want a better, healthier, and happier life for yourself.

A key element of successful grief work is being able to express freely your thoughts and feelings. In addition to talking to someone, many divorced persons find journaling enormously helpful and therapeutic. In a journal, you can safely pour out the feelings, thoughts, and attitudes you have related to your divorce; no one need read what you've written except you.

Exercise also helps. Shawn, a young man in his early thirties who went through a traumatic divorce, agrees completely. "I found that plain old walking took the edge off the pain. When I first started walking, I was so badly out of shape that I only lasted about ten minutes, then collapsed. Now I walk three miles a day—rain or shine.

"I discovered that walking is great for loneliness. When I walk down the street, people smile and wave, and sometimes I stop and chat. I don't feel nearly as alone when I walk, and the exercise clears my mind and helps me think better."

If you find yourself grieving from the experience of divorce, be gentle, self-forgiving, and extra kind to yourself. You do not need more condemnation. Work on accepting yourself and letting go of the grief.

No one can tell you how to grieve or how long to grieve. We each grieve in our own unique way and at our own pace. However, grieving too long can become counterproductive, unhealthy, and even self-destructive.

How do we know it's time to end our grieving? When we feel a need to get on with our lives. If we cannot eventually move in this direction, we risk becoming victims and not survivors. The grief then threatens to overtake us.

Grieving and Prayer

Prayer is a valuable tool in dealing with grief. Prayer helps heal even the deepest grief. Sometimes, praying for the healing of your grief necessitates praying for your former spouse, asking God to bless him or her, and being willing to forgive that person and yourself. This can be extremely difficult, but it is often the key to emotional freedom and the final resolution of the grief process.

With God's help, the help of others, and drawing upon your own inner resources, you can do it. One day it will dawn on you that your grieving is finished; you'll sense peace. That kind of personal resurrection is worth working toward with all the energy and hope you can muster.

The Quest for Intimacy

In the Book of Genesis, God forever underscored the social nature of the human being: "It is not good that the man should be alone; I will make him a helper as his partner" (2:18). God implanted within us a desire for unity, companionship, and closeness with other human beings.

You may have spent many years searching for a suitable partner, and once you found that person, married him or her. What is particularly disappointing about divorce is the realization that the person you selected as your partner was not the one destined to stay by your side for a lifetime.

And even though you may still be hurting as a result of your marriage coming to an end, it is nonetheless possible that at some level you have already begun to search for another suitable partner. In your heart, you know you want to try again to establish a bond of closeness with another human being. That state of being close is called intimacy.

The Second Vatican Council viewed intimacy as a crucial ingredient of marriage. It even described marriage as an "intimate union of persons."

Even without marriage, we human beings are drawn to the experience of intimacy. We tend to resist isolation and aloneness, instinctively knowing that too much of either is not good for us. The quest for intimacy is fundamentally a quest to be known, to be loved and accepted for who and what we are, and to be connected to some other person at a deep and enduring level.

An "intimate union of persons" inside or outside of marriage is no minor achievement. It takes time and considerable effort on the part of both persons involved. Sadly, the quest for intimacy is often and easily sabotaged by something disguised as intimacy—sex. Polly learned how physical expressions of affection can be far from genuine intimacy.

"After my divorce I was absolutely starved for an intimate relationship, so I speeded up the process, thinking everything would fall into place eventually. Believe me, it didn't.

"I became sexually intimate with a man I had known only a

short time but who seemed to be a perfect companion and a good choice for remarriage. We rushed headlong into the sexual aspect of the relationship and short-circuited everything else. We didn't take the time to put down a good foundation based on respect, trust, communication, understanding, and simple friendship. So when the romantic part started to cool down, as invariably it does, there was nothing present to sustain us.

"We had no difficulty achieving sexual intimacy—that was the easy part. But really connecting—becoming best friends and soul mates—just never happened. It's really sad; if we had just been friends first—good friends—I think we could have grown very close and would have known real intimacy."

God designed each of us as a sexual being. However, as Polly indicates, a sexual relationship with another person and genuine intimacy are not the same thing.

Another common mistake is confusing sex with love. Dennis can vouch for that.

"Following my divorce, I must have dated twenty women in a span of two years. I was empty and aching inside from the loss of my wife and family. I used sex to fill that void, all the while pretending it was love.

"In the back of my mind, though, I knew I was lying to myself; I knew it wasn't love at all. At best, it was lust. It wasn't fair to the women who were looking for a decent stable life with someone. And it wasn't fair to me.

"I misused sex—but finally came to the realization that it was both wrong and sinful.

"I'll tell you what turned my thinking around. I made a good confession. I happened to stop in a church one day for a little quiet time alone and noticed an elderly priest hearing confessions.

"I hadn't been to confession in probably ten years or more,

but something made me get up and enter the confessional, which had a sign on it reading 'Reconciliation Room.' I wasn't even sure what that meant, but I went inside and talked to the priest face to face.

"He was gentle but firm and called me back to a sense of moral responsibility that I had so sadly lacked following my divorce. That was all it took, although I must say that in my soul I knew I was ready to change. I just had denied it for quite some time until God caught up to me.

"Now I'm working on my annulment, and I don't plan to do any dating until it is completed. I just want to work on myself."

When it comes to meeting your intimacy needs, no blueprint provides all the answers. Here are some general guidelines that have proven helpful to others who have faced the same issues you're probably facing now.

Intimacy begins with yourself. Amid the turbulence of your divorce, you may have lost touch with yourself, becoming self-estranged and alienated from the person you once knew. Anger, guilt, denial, and the repression/suppression of other strong feelings can bring this about.

So start with yourself. Take the time to rediscover the person you really are at your deepest level. Reestablish a sense of being close with yourself before you rush headlong into a relationship with someone else.

Be gentle, caring, and forgiving toward yourself. Be good to yourself, but also be completely honest. Take a thorough look at those areas of your life that you may have ignored or neglected along the way. Give a great deal of attention to your relationship with God. As you move closer to God and come to better understand that person who is authentically you, you will find yourself far more capable of sharing deeply with another human being. In this way, self-intimacy makes possible all other forms of intimacy.

Love yourself. Jesus wisely associated the love of self with love of others because the latter becomes impossible without the former.

To love yourself means you have a fundamental sense of your value, dignity, and self-worth. It means you respect yourself and are unwilling to do anything that will cause you to lose either your self-respect or your integrity.

Accept self-responsibility. Self-love goes hand in hand with self-responsibility. When you love and care for yourself, you consciously recognize that you and you alone are responsible for your behaviors. Consequently, you are careful to choose those behaviors that enhance and enrich your life rather than engaging in those that jeopardize your well-being.

Genuine self-love is the opposite of selfishness and narcissism; it is an excessive preoccupation with oneself that makes a person unable to care about the needs of others. Persons who love themselves and know themselves well are far better able to reach out in service to others. Their comfort level with themselves is high. They do not expect someone else to fulfill all their needs for love and acceptance because they love and accept themselves just the way they are.

If you feel you do not adequately love yourself, make this the number one goal of your life; begin working toward it today. Saint John of the Cross once said that where there is no love, put love, and you will find love. As you begin investing love in yourself, you will be far better equipped to love others.

Give yourself the gift of time. When it comes to the quest for intimacy, do not accelerate the process; decelerate it. Give yourself plenty of time to work toward the goals identified in this chapter—a deeper appreciation of yourself, healthier self-love, and genuine friendships with others.

Following a divorce, many persons have a kind of "deprivation mentality." They feel so deprived of intimacy that they're willing to take huge risks to fulfill their needs. Many of these risks, however, are counterproductive, futile, and can actually be dangerous and self-destructive.

One marriage counselor suggests to his clients who have just ended a marriage that they allow sufficient time for grieving and healing. He feels that this process takes at least a year; for some, it will take longer.

Initially, think in terms of developing new friendships with a variety of persons, both women and men. This will provide you with people to talk to and share with and will take the edge off your loneliness.

No matter how impatient or needy you feel, there is no way to hasten the process leading to genuine intimacy. It will bloom like a flower in its own season when the conditions are right— and when it appears, you will know it.

Chapter Three

From Pain to Peace

Catholics who go through a divorce often discover a need to work through a number of important spiritual issues with both God and the Church. The one is basically inseparable from the other.

When it comes to God, two prevailing feelings that frequently need attention are guilt and anger. Guilt usually stems from the belief that by getting a divorce you have somehow failed God and others. Anger may come from the feeling that God let you down by not intervening to save your marriage. David's and Shirley's stories exemplify each of these emotions.

David: "When my marriage ended, I went through a phase of deep guilt and remorse. The fact is I knew in my heart that I had not worked hard enough on the relationship with my wife and that our marriage could probably have been salvaged if I had.

"I felt so shameful about not trying harder that it affected my relationship with God. I began to feel that I had let God down. That made me feel even more miserable, and pretty soon it was as though I had committed the sin against the Holy Spirit and could not be forgiven. I actually came to believe I had committed a heinous, unpardonable sin by divorcing.

"Things got much worse before they got better. The guilt and shame drove me away from both God and the Church. Even though I was able to receive the sacraments, I chose not to because of my tremendous sense of unworthiness.

"I felt God needed to punish me for what I had done, so I started to believe something terrible was going to happen to me or my children. The whole thing got way out of hand, and I completely lost my spiritual balance. I was well on the way to a major nervous breakdown."

What turned things around for David?

"It was the sacrament of reconciliation—and it happened in the most unusual way. I went to see my dentist, and there in the waiting room was my pastor, who had also come to have some work done on his teeth. We chatted and he remarked that he hadn't seen me in church for a long time. Well, right then and there in that waiting room I started to unload my spiritual baggage. Thank the Lord we were the only two there!

"Afterward, he invited me over to the rectory for a cup of coffee and more talk. Before I left that afternoon, he heard my confession. All my life I've been afraid of dentists, but from that day on I've been glad they exist. Because of that 'chance' encounter in the dentist's office, I was able to get my spiritual life back on track—and I think my mind was saved as well."

Shirley: "I was angry! I divorced God as well as my husband. I know it sounds strange, but it's true. Right to the end of my failing marriage, I expected God to do something miraculous. I wanted some kind of divine intervention that would make everything right again. When I didn't get my miracle, I decided that the relationship between God and me was over.

"I stopped going to church, stopped praying, and stopped doing anything religious. My attitude must have been contagious because my kids went right along with me. The whole family climbed aboard the bandwagon I had created out of my anger. We became your classic fallen-away, alienated Catholics."

How did Shirley resolve her dispute with God?

"The resolution didn't come right away. Two years passed and I found myself missing God. Christmas and Easter were meaningless, and inside of me there was a kind of nagging, lonely feeling that nothing else and nobody else could satisfy.

"Finally, I couldn't take it anymore. I went to an Advent communal penance service and poured my heart out to God. I told God I was still mad but couldn't live without him. I also admitted to God and to myself that no miracle could have saved our marriage; right from the beginning, my former husband never really wanted to share life with me.

"I guess I felt like the prodigal daughter coming home, but it wasn't a bad feeling at all. In fact, for the first time in years, I experienced deep peace and joy."

Shirley admits, "I may have divorced God, but God never divorced me. God never abandoned me either. God was there all the time, waiting for me to come home. It's hard to stay angry at someone who treats you so well. Needless to say, I'm not angry at God anymore."

You and God

Because divorce often brings much turbulence and chaos, it is not unusual to experience some dramatic upheavals in your spiritual life. Keep in mind that divorce is not an unforgivable sin; it need not alienate you or separate you from God. The end of a relationship with another human being should not and must not mean the end of your relationship with God.

God loves us and accepts us even when we fail. God's love is completely unconditional. Yet it is not uncommon to make God the scapegoat and blame him for letting us down, as Shirley did. The end result may be deep anger or even rage.

What should you do if you're angry at God following the experience of your divorce? Treat your anger in the same way you would if you were angry at any other person. First admit and acknowledge your anger. Don't pretend you're not angry at God when you really are. Own up to it and talk directly to God about your feelings: "God, I'm very mad at you and here's why."

Then, instead of holding onto your anger, reconcile as soon as possible. Without swift reconciling, the anger may contaminate every aspect of your spiritual life. You may actually have to forgive God for what you perceive to be unfairness or injustice toward you. You should also ask for forgiveness of your anger directed toward God.

These reconciliatory steps may have to be repeated over and over until your anger is dissipated. The sacrament of reconciliation is an excellent way to do this. A good confessor can facilitate genuine peacemaking between yourself and God and can help bring about inner healing.

Just keep in mind that God can handle even our angriest feelings. God is the one who placed this powerful emotion within us, knowing full well there would be times when we would use it against him.

In itself, anger is never wrong or sinful. It is what we do with it that matters a great deal. If we deliberately hold onto it, feed it, and allow it to poison every aspect of our lives, we can expect serious spiritual and emotional pain.

Anger and guilt have powerfully obsessive features that make them difficult to eliminate from our lives. If you're wrestling with these strong emotions following your divorce, seek help from someone competent in these psycho-spiritual matters.

You and the Church

After divorcing, most Catholics are likely to view the process of making things right with God as integrally linked to making things right with the Church. The two tend to be inseparable. Sometimes the process is impeded by misinformation. Scott's story is sadly familiar—especially to many priests.

"Following my divorce I was given some erroneous information by a family member that torpedoed me spiritually for the next three years. I was told that I could not celebrate the sacraments because I was divorced. I had not remarried at that point and had no intention of remarrying, so there were no impediments at all to the sacraments, but unfortunately, I believed what I heard.

"It was not until I happened to read an article on divorce in a Catholic periodical that I realized how badly misinformed I had been. I was angry at the family member who fed me the wrong information, but most of all I was angry at myself for not taking the time to check with my pastor, who could have told me what Church law really does say."

In and of itself, divorce does not prevent a Catholic from celebrating the sacraments. Excommunication is never the issue, even if remarriage takes place outside the Church. The practice of annulments is a crucial issue, however, and warrants at least brief attention here.

A divorce means that a marriage has been ended in a civil court of law. A Church annulment means that a competent Catholic Church authority, generally called a matrimonial tribunal, has determined that a marriage in question is null and void; that is, it was not a true marital covenant. Unless there are other impediments, the persons obtaining the annulment are free to remarry in the Church.

There was a time in the history of the Church when annulments were rare. Now they're fairly common. In her reflection upon what constitutes a true marriage covenant, the Church has come to realize that certain factors sometimes may be present that actually prevent such a covenant from taking place. Some of these factors are psychological in nature. Mental and emotional disorders, for example, can render a person incapable of a lasting marital relationship. Other psychological concerns are linked to alcoholism, drug addiction, severe immaturity, or perhaps a person's inability or incapacity to fulfill the commitments that go with marriage.

There are other factors that block or prevent a true marital covenant from ever taking place. These may include an intention against having children; against fidelity; or against a permanent, lasting relationship.

It isn't uncommon for tribunals to review cases where a person married to escape an unhappy home or where a couple felt forced to marry because of a pregnancy. In both situations, marriage was employed as a solution to a problem, not as a covenant freely entered. Annulments are usually granted in such cases.

Once a civil divorce has been obtained, an annulment can then be sought. Annulment procedures vary somewhat from diocese to diocese. Generally, the way to begin is to contact a priest in your parish. You will be given a questionnaire/petition with specific directions. For example, you may be asked to provide a copy of your baptismal certificate, marriage license, and decree of divorce. You will also be required to describe in some detail why your marriage failed.

In addition to the written information, some tribunals may request a personal interview with you to obtain more data and to pastorally provide you with an opportunity to discuss your marriage and divorce with a Church representative.

As part of the annulment process, you will be asked to list the names of witnesses who can offer an opinion—usually in writing as to why your marriage failed. A witness may be a family member, friend, or acquaintance. Expert witnesses such as marriage counselors or psychologists will require a release-of-information form signed by you.

Annulment procedures do require that your former spouse be contacted so that his or her viewpoint about the marriage may be obtained. If he or she refuses to cooperate, the process still moves forward until a decision is reached.

In many dioceses there is no cost for an annulment. Some dioceses may charge a modest processing fee to help defray costs. There is no way to "buy" a Church annulment.

The time period for an annulment tends to be minimally a year. Complicated cases may require more time in order to gather evidence and render a decision. On occasion, some cases may have to be abandoned if there is a severe lack of evidence.

If you are a Catholic who was married outside the Church, is presently divorced, and is considering remarriage, a formal annulment case may not be necessary. Yours may be a relatively simple kind of marriage case called a lack-of-form case that is uncomplicated and rapidly processed. Check with your parish priest to find out.

Annulments are not meant to be exercises in cutting red tape to free an individual to remarry in the Church; they are not "Catholic divorces." They are signs of the Church's compassion and concern for those who have gone through the experience of divorce. They can be an invaluable means to facilitate healing and assist in the rebuilding of a new life.

Many Catholics who have gone through an annulment have stated that they felt the Church was truly listening to them and their needs. Others say that the annulment process finally enabled them to leave the past behind with dignity and move forward into their futures with a sense of peace about their lives.

When it comes to divorce, both God and the Church are primarily concerned with forgiveness, reconciliation, healing, and renewal. As you discover this to be true, may your healing enable you to embrace a future filled with the promise of peace and hope.

You and the Community

The old saying, "Pain is inevitable, misery is optional," seems to apply in a special way to the experience of divorce. For many, if not most persons, divorce is an excruciatingly painful life event. However, it does not mean a life sentence to a miserable existence without any chance of parole. Pain during one phase of our lives does not have to mean we are doomed to suffer forever.

There are community resources that can serve as shock absorbers; they can help cushion the emotional blows of divorce. Their effectiveness depends on how well and how consistently you avail yourself of them. Seriously consider the following means of community support.

Individual and family counseling. Just a few counseling sessions, with or without your children, sometimes can work wonders. Talking to a trained professional greatly facilitates healing.

Remember, however, that therapists are not magicians; they cannot magically resolve all your problems. They are trained to help you identify and clarify the major issues you need to address. They then remain available to assist you as you make decisions about these issues.

Therapy can help restore a sense of balance to your emotional life following a divorce. It is an especially effective way to process deep-seated anger and guilt. Heather found this to be true.

"Getting into counseling after my divorce was the smartest decision I could have made. My pastor told me about the counseling available through Catholic Charities, so I made an appointment with a therapist who had a lot of experience helping people cope with the adjustment problems associated with divorce. The counselor was wonderful. I felt I could tell her anything and everything about my life. She first helped me 'frame the issues,' as she called it. Together we looked at the areas I needed to work on.

"One really big area was my intense fear of making it on my own. The counselor pointed out that I would be receiving both alimony and child support. That guaranteed income would provide some financial protection and would give me options I might not have had otherwise. She suggested a part-time job that would enable me to go back to school—and that's exactly what I did. I'm now a nurse in a large hospital and doing very well.

"My two children were eight and ten at the time of my divorce. I took them to two sessions during which they got a chance to articulate some of their own anger about what had happened.

"One of the things I had worried about was the cost for counseling. But the cost was manageable. The fee was based on a sliding scale related to my income, so it didn't cost me an arm and a leg. However, I want to say that the counseling would have been worth it at any price. It was the biggest single factor in helping my children and me heal rapidly from the divorce experience. It especially helped me make peace with my past."

For a reputable therapist, check the Yellow Pages of your telephone directory under "Mental Health Services." Both community mental-health agencies as well as Catholic Charities often base their fees on ability to pay. Private agencies and private practitioners usually charge a higher fee. When you call, ask about fees so you won't be surprised later. Also, be as specific as you can about the kind of help you're looking for so you are linked to a therapist familiar with your particular issues.

Remember that many clergy and parish staff members have a background in divorce counseling. Check with your local parish to see what resources they provide. Perhaps the parish will suggest someone in the community who comes highly recommended as a counselor.

Support groups: Many communities have a variety of support groups tailored to different needs—Alcoholics Anonymous (AA), Al-Anon, Narcotics Anonymous (NA), Overeaters Anonymous (OA), Adult Children of Alcoholics (ACOA), and Parents Without Partners (PWP). These groups can be extremely beneficial in helping a person cope with issues linked to divorce.

Some communities offer support groups for the separated, divorcing, and divorced. These can be particularly helpful in providing persons with an opportunity to talk out their feelings in a safe and nonjudgmental setting, thus expanding their coping skills. Such a group can actually become a kind of surrogate family, offering the love, understanding, and nurturing that is enormously healing and restorative.

Cindy couldn't find such a support group in her community. Her solution was to start one. "I read everything I could find on the subject of divorce and listened to dozens of tapes to prepare myself to get a group going. My pastor gave me permission to use the church basement and to put a notice in the church bulletin.

"I expected about half a dozen people that first night. But twenty-seven people came, and eventually we ended up with two groups—one meeting on a weekday evening, the other on the weekend.

"I shared with the group my visions about the importance of healing together. I strongly felt that the meetings wouldn't work and might even self-destruct if we turned them into pity parties or complaint sessions. We all needed to address the issue of self-healing following our divorces, and I felt that we had to maintain that focus.

"Because the groups began on a positive note, they've lasted. It's been three years now, and they're still going strong. Many men and women have benefited from these support-group meetings. From the beginning, the key concepts that have acted like rudders have been 'support' and 'healing.' Put them together and you have an unbeatable combination that really helps persons struggling with the fallout from a divorce."

Spiritual resources: "I tried very hard to make God the third person in our marriage," recalls Linda, who has been divorced for two years. "But my former husband put up too many roadblocks. However, God certainly became the third person in our divorce. I know beyond a shadow of a doubt that without God's help, I would not have made it."

Linda's conviction is echoed by many who have gone through the experience of divorce. Leaning on God for support and help is the lifeline that sustains countless numbers of divorced persons—even those who may have had only a lukewarm relationship with God when things were going well.

"I ignored God the entire time I was married," Rod comments, shaking his head. "But I rediscovered him quickly during my divorce. At first, I prayed just to survive and for no other reason. Then, when I did survive, I started to pray out of gratitude. In a way now, I'm almost glad my divorce took place. It provided me with the kick in the pants I needed to go back to God. And you know what? I found God was waiting patiently for me all the time. I may have left God, but God never left me or gave up on me, and I know he never will."

A strong spiritual life is a powerful shock absorber during any crisis, especially a divorce. Draw upon all the spiritual resources available to you. These are likely to include frequent celebration of the sacraments, personal and community prayer, Scripture reading, worshiping with others, meditation, retreats, a Beginning Experience Weekend, Bible study groups, and anything else that enables you to feel more intimately connected to God and that provides you with the spiritual strength you need to carry on. This is often discovered in community with others.

God has a plan for your life. Now that you're divorced, you need to know more than ever what that plan is. You find out through prayer and quiet discernment. Pray for the gifts of the Holy Spirit, especially wisdom and courage. Pray daily that you may be guided, directed, and inspired to make good decisions for yourself and your family.

The famous spiritual prescription, "Let go and let God," becomes particularly appropriate in connection with divorce. Instead of trying to tell God what the solutions for your problems should be, try turning things over to God's providential care.

Surrender yourself and let God truly be the manager of your new life. As you voluntarily give up some of the control of your life to God, you will be surprised at how much peace and serenity you receive. You will discover that not only is God the Higher Power but also the Higher Friend who walks with you through every circumstance of your new life.

God is always on the side of healing—your healing. Asking for God's loving, healing, and restoring touch upon your life is one major way to facilitate your own personal renewal following a divorce.

You and Your Own Resources

Do not overlook yourself as a major source of strength during this time. You are not defeated or ruined. Affirm yourself and draw on your own inner strengths. Pay attention to the emotions that flood through you. They will not manage and control you if you work hard at managing them.

Anger and guilt have been identified as two major emotions associated with divorce. There are others, such as anxiety and depression. Anxiety tends to be rooted in the feeling of being threatened by fear of the future and what will befall you. Depression arises from a sense of loss. It usually brings with it two other potent feelings—hopelessness and helplessness.

Both anxiety and depression should not be ignored. They can easily create a state of emotional paralysis that results in an inability to function well. A person struggling with either anxiety or depression (and often both are present at the same time) may be unable to make even the simplest decisions and, for all practical purposes, will be rendered dysfunctional.

If you feel you're being incapacitated by these or other powerful emotions and do not feel your own strengths can sustain you, seek help. Begin with your doctor or a mental-health professional who is trained to assess your situation and help you understand and master your out-of-control emotions. Talking to someone about your feelings and emotions is a good way to regain control over them. As you successfully manage these emotions, you will feel more in command of your own life. You will be able to make responsible decisions and take the initiatives necessary to meet the challenges of your new life.

Finally, take good care of yourself. The period before, during, and after a divorce is usually traumatic and highly stressful. You are the best person equipped to know how to take care of yourself, and this means attending to basics—getting enough sleep, eating properly, and learning how to unwind and relax.

Because of the high levels of stress associated with divorce, it is tempting to resort to alcohol, tranquilizers, or other kinds of drugs in an attempt to cope. Use of alcohol and other means of coping can gradually render you more dysfunctional as your dependency upon them increases. If you find yourself struggling with substance abuse or addictive behavior of any kind, reach out for help. Talk to your physician or a trained counselor who can provide suggestions and put you on the road leading to self-healing.

Exercise is an important and highly effective means of coping. Connie just came through a painful divorce and underscores this in her remarks. "During my divorce, people would tell me that I seemed to be coping well. I told them it was simple. Each day, rain or shine, I ran ten miles. I even ran on Christmas day during a blizzard. I realize that not everyone can do this, but the rigorous exercise program I set for myself helped me bum off bad feelings. When the divorce was finalized, my grieving was pretty much over and I went about the business of rebuilding my life."

Draw upon any and every supportive resource available to you during this stressful time—including those within yourself. Stretch yourself and take some chances as you strive for healing. The art class you've always wanted to take may do you a world of good. A part-time or full-time job will help you feel more financially secure. Joining the bowling league may help you get rid of some major frustrations. Chopping wood may be a good way to work off anger.

Pain may be inevitable with a divorce; misery truly is optional. Don't stew in your own juices. Pursue personal healing and a sense of peace as rapidly and vigorously as you can. Stick with the process until your healing is complete—no matter how long it takes.

Chapter Four

From Darkness to Light

Time passes. You feel yourself changing. The long emotional winter begins to come to an end, and there are signs of spring in your life. You feel lighter, more together, and at peace with yourself. The pain in your mind and spirit may still remain, but it's manageable now and far less crippling.

You start to think of yourself as another Lazarus being summoned from the darkness of your tomb to a new life and new beginnings. You begin to feel whole again.

With these awakenings and recognitions come exhilarating feelings of hope and restoration. Roger explains it this way: "It must have been about ten months after my divorce, an extremely painful divorce that brought on a depression and despair I had never known before. I remember it was a Sunday morning because I dragged myself out of bed to go to Mass.

"After Mass, I realized that something was different. I didn't know what it was at first, and then it hit me. The darkness I had experienced was gone! I felt joyous and alive. Although it was late autumn, it seemed like Easter Sunday inside of me. I knew then that I was going to make it."

One Day at a Time

The first and most basic recognition often is the fact that you have survived the divorce. You have passed through an emotional and spiritual hurricane and are still here. As a survivor, you have not only made it but also will continue to make it one day at a time.

With your sense of survivorship comes the additional recognition that your grieving, for the most part, is over. You have reached that all-important stage of acceptance.

There may still be twinges of pain and anger when you think back on certain aspects of what's happened to you, but your emotions no longer control you. Your mental health is much better. You may still have some difficulty forgiving a former spouse who hurt or damaged you in some way, but you are determined to forgive yourself—and you know you will.

Another sign of new life is the positive feelings you begin to have about yourself. Day by day you feel more like caring for and nurturing yourself. You start to like yourself as a person and it feels good.

"I knew I was coming back to the land of the living," says Clara, "when I glanced at myself in the mirror one day and said, 'You need a completely new look.'

"I made an appointment at the beauty parlor and got a new hair style and a manicure. I also went on a diet and lost twenty pounds. People started telling me I looked ten years younger. Believe me, it was such a glorious feeling to get positive strokes after all the negativity associated with my divorce."

Still another sign of acceptance and healing may be a growing sense of self-esteem and self-worth. You are learning to see yourself as a good person. Integrity and self-respect are very important issues for you now.

You have also separated the failure of the marriage from who you are as a person. You no longer believe that just because the marriage failed, you are a failure as well. The love and acceptance you've invested in yourself are now paying off handsomely; you readily acknowledge that you are not a failure as a human being. Much of your self-pity is gone, and you start to relate to yourself as you would to your best friend.

More than ever you're aware of the need for balance in your life. You recognize that you have certain needs and that others have certain needs. You want to reach out and help others as much as you can without overextending yourself or neglecting your own needs—as you may have done in the past.

Starting Over

Along with these awakenings comes a dawning sense that it is time to start over—to begin again. This doesn't mean running headlong into a new relationship that will eventually lead to remarriage. Remarriage is not likely to be the primary issue. Starting over means taking a good look at yourself: "Who am I and what do I need right now?"

That's what Paula did. "Within six months after my divorce, men were asking me out on dates. Even my two grown children encouraged me to say yes. I guess they recognized that I was lonely and craved companionship.

"But you know what I did? I turned down every offer. Something deep inside told me that I just wasn't ready to date. I didn't need another exclusive relationship with a man. What I really needed were new friends."

Paula chuckles. "So I joined a swimming class with a group of other women. While I was married, I had almost no women friends, and I missed that. I was determined to make some female friends and, by golly, I did. Close friends, too. I'll soon be leaving for two weeks in Hawaii with three members of our swimming group and I couldn't be more excited!"

As these changes within you indicate that you are coming out of the darkness into the light, it's all right to focus primarily on yourself and what you want and need. By no means is this selfish. It is absolutely crucial if you are going to build a meaningful future for yourself.

Assess and reassess your goals. For example, is this a good time to start looking at new career or educational opportunities? If you can't go back to school full time, consider taking a class in some area of life enrichment. If not an academic class, what about an aerobics class? The exercise will make you feel good and help you function better.

You now know that the primary responsibility for your life rests squarely in your hands. You may have occasional fantasies about finding a new mate who will take care of you, but you also realize that it may not happen. You have to take care of yourself, and that's a worthy purpose. With God's help and opening yourself to the support of others, you can do just that and have a healthy and satisfying life.

At this stage of growth, you don't feel as helpless or hopeless as you may have during and immediately after your divorce. You now have a sense that your life can improve and become better, and you're willing to take some of the risks that will make that possible.

Yet you also know that you have to be realistic. There is only so much you can accomplish in the immediate moment with the resources available to you. You are trying hard to be more firmly grounded in reality, and more than ever you are willing to take a good look at your boundaries and limitations: "Here is where I start, and here is where I stop." Following a divorce, the tendency is to push far beyond one's boundaries to a point that is both unreasonable and unhealthy. You are determined to avoid doing this at all costs. It's all part of your new determination to take care of yourself.

As you prepare to venture further into your new life, it is a good idea to be somewhat cautious and careful. Many roads beckon, but you cannot travel all of them. Carefully evaluate where you want to go and what you want to do. Get as much feedback and input from trusted others as you can.

If you've sought counseling, talk over your needs and aspirations with your therapist. Utilize all your support systems as sounding boards to test new ideas and possibilities. Research those areas that especially interest you.

"A year or so after my divorce, I decided I wanted to be a high-school science teacher," recalls Gene. "I didn't really know how feasible my goal was, so I visited several high schools in different cities and talked to both the principals and the science teachers on staff.

"They strongly encouraged me. They pointed out that the market for science teachers was expanding, especially as older teachers retired. On the basis of what I heard from them, I made my decision to return to school. Next fall I'll be teaching full time."

If you're thinking of radically restructuring your life and making major lifestyle changes (quitting your job, selling your home, moving), avoid acting impulsively. Analyze your situation carefully; weigh all the pros and cons. This may not be a good time to take unnecessary gambles with high stakes involved. Protect yourself at all costs.

Learn to view your life as a gradual unfolding, a process rather than an endless series of goals to be achieved or tasks to accomplish. Enjoy not only your life but also yourself and the person you are. You are worth loving; you are worth liking. As you start over, it's important that you like yourself a great deal.

Do What You Love...

A popular self-help book was titled, *Do What You Love and the Money Will Follow*. It was a philosophy I have upheld all my career life, especially since I am involved in ministry. The money is still catching up to the "do what I love" part.

Recently, however, someone suggested, "Do what you love and *love* will follow." How does that happen? A close friend, Ellie, said when she was going through her divorce her Catholic singles group told her how important it was to participate in the "social rituals" of dating. And so she found herself sitting in smoky, loud bars with her Catholic single peers and wishing she were home and feeling very sorry for herself. After the third time she said, "This is silly. I never enjoyed this lifestyle when I was married. Why would I suddenly enjoy this social ritual now?" And she thanked the group and left. With the new time her singleness had created, she enrolled in a few botanical courses, joined a book club, and found out it was true. She was in love!

Does that mean that Prince Charming was lurking in the greenhouse? Maybe. When we are involved with people who share similar interests we are more likely to find the basis of friendship. By now, given our own experience of both successes and missteps, we should be well aware that the foundation for a lifelong relationship is built on the rules of friendship. What better way to begin than in discovering our similarities?

Do what you love also opens us up to the necessity of learning who we are, as individuals. When we find out what turns us on, we become astounded at how unique we are, how wonderfully made we are. When we discover the gifts God gave us, we are most likely to begin to love ourselves, maybe for the first time.

It is not the new haircut, the color consultant, the body-building routine that makes us attractive to others. It is the signal we send out that says we are made just as God intended that makes a new glow from within, that brings the love that is waiting to follow.

As for Ellie's new love? "Love God. Love your neighbor as yourself." Learning to love ourselves is the best way to attract others.

God and Your Future

As you look at new horizons and ponder untraveled roads, don't forget God. Strengthen your relationship with God; ask God to go before you into your future and give you the faith to courageously follow. Ask God to gift you with those individuals you need and who need you so your life may evolve into a balance of both giving and receiving. Invite God to use you to bring more love, compassion, understanding, and goodness to our world. Let God co-create with you a new and better life so you avoid the mistakes of the past and begin building a meaningful present and future.

You know you cannot create a new life for yourself or by yourself. You need God and others. Recognize and acknowledge that, and then go ahead. With a heart full of trust, take God's hand and walk toward a bright and promising future.

Remarriage

One indisputable sign that there is life after divorce is seen in the fact that the majority of divorced persons eventually remarry.

Five out of six men who have been divorced will remarry, as will three out of four divorced women. Men tend to remarry more quickly than do women. Approximately half of those who divorce will remarry another divorced person.

Unfortunately, however, remarriage is hardly a guarantee of happiness or even a lifelong relationship. The sad fact is that second marriages fail at a 25 percent higher rate than first marriages.

Therapists who work with problems associated with remarriage point out that a major reason for the high failure of second marriages is that people too often remarry for the wrong reasons. What are some of those wrong reasons?

Loneliness. "After my divorce," recalls Gwen, "I was so lonely I could hardly stand it. In fact, I actually became afraid of my loneliness. I couldn't bear being alone, so I threw myself into a whirlwind of activities that served to distract me.

"I also became reckless and indiscriminate in my relationships, dating men just to have someone to be with. I married Jack because he was a lot of fun and I didn't feel lonely when I was with him. I can hardly believe it—I married him after knowing him only four months. It was simply a terrible mistake!

"After the marriage, I realized that we had almost nothing in common, at least not enough to sustain a lifelong relationship. The initial attraction was not strong enough to carry the marriage, the result being there wasn't enough 'glue' to hold us together. Eventually, the whole thing came crashing down around our ears.

"My advice? Don't even use the word *remarriage* for a minimum of a year after your divorce. Give yourself plenty of time to heal and to evaluate carefully your new relationships. Slow yourself down. You'll be far less likely to make the mistakes I did.

And keep in mind that loneliness won't kill you. It may hurt, but the pain can prove to be a lot less devastating than the pain of a bad relationship."

Looking for a parenting partner: Divorced persons with children often make the mistake of marrying to find a father or mother figure for the family. The trap here may be one of basic incompatibility between the new parent and the children, leading to clashes that strain the marriage.

In addition, if both adults have children of their own from a prior marriage, the blending of two families may prove to be a formidable task or may not be accomplished at all. The result will be severe stresses on the new marriage relationship and perhaps the failure of the two spouses to bond adequately to each other.

Lack of psychological autonomy: Psychological autonomy is the emotional ability to stand on our own two feet. It recognizes how important relationships are, but at the same time, it prevents our identity from being swallowed up or destroyed by another person.

If we are psychologically autonomous, our world does not have to end when a close relationship ends. Even if we find ourselves alone, we can still create a rich, satisfying life of our own. We can continue to live instead of self-destructing.

Persons who feel they must remarry because they cannot be a whole person without a spouse are not psychologically autonomous. Because of their neediness, they will likely find themselves in a relationship that is neither healthy nor fulfilling.

Dependency: Divorced persons who remarry because they are looking for a spouse to cook their meals, do the cleaning and laundry, mow the grass, and take care of the house are asking for trouble. Basically, they are looking for someone to take care of them.

Because of their dependency needs, they are likely to be less cautious and objective in their assessment of a relationship, and this can lead to serious problems. A husband who is a terrific handyman and a wife who is a superb cook are great blessings. But in themselves they are not crucial to a healthy marriage. You're likely to be far better off hiring someone to do these chores rather than marrying someone to do them. The cost in the first scenario will almost certainly be considerably less than the price you pay in the second.

What, then, are key components to weigh in the decision to remarry?

Mutual spiritual discernment: A believing Christian should have some sense that God is calling him or her to a lifelong, life-giving relationship with a special man or woman. Equally important is the same discernment by the other partner. It is crucial that both adults have a sense of where they stand with God, both individually and as a couple. In this manner, God becomes Lord of the marriage—that all-important third partner.

Kristin agrees completely. "A major reason why my second marriage has done so well is that both Sam and I have a strong faith in God and share that faith freely with each other. We have built our marriage on a true spiritual foundation—something I was unable to do in my first marriage. Sam and I reap the benefits of our relationship with God in our own relationship on a daily basis. We're so grateful that God brought us together. We've been blessed beyond our expectations, and we bless God in return."

Maturity: Maturity is the ability to handle the good, the bad, the joys, and the sorrows that go with every relationship without giving up or running away. Mature adults put off instant gratification for long-term gain. They do not have to get their own way; they know how to compromise. When they're wrong, they can admit it.

Mature spouses are responsible for themselves, as well as for each other. They're dependable. Their actions match their words. They are unselfish and can freely serve both their spouse and other family members without bitterness or anger.

Two mature adults stand a strong chance of making a marriage relationship work. Two immature persons or a combination of one mature and one immature partner will have a difficult time in marriage.

Good communication: Poor communication is usually cited as a major reason for the decline and failure of marriages. This comes as no surprise; communication fuels a relationship and deepens love, trust, and acceptance. It creates an environment and an attitude that says, "You can talk to me about anything whatsoever and I will still love you."

The best kind of communication is honest, direct, and open. It is largely based on the sharing and self-disclosure of one partner which in turn invites a similar response from the other.

Through deep sharing, the couple grows together because each person continually learns something new about the other. Because of this, there is no opportunity for stagnation to creep into the relationship—it flourishes.

"A major reason why I wanted to marry Nancy," admits Steven, "was the fact that we could talk about anything and everything with each other. There are no 'red flag' areas that we have to avoid in our conversations.

"Believe me, that was definitely not the case in my first marriage. My former wife and I tiptoed around certain things that later came to plague us with a vengeance.

"Talking is probably one of the most healing things a couple can do. When you talk to the person you love, you feel connected. You feel like you belong to someone. You both feel good, and that's good for the relationship."

Companionship: Couples who enjoy each other's company do much better in marriage. Companionship is that comfort level which allows you to recognize, appreciate, and celebrate the simple things—a quiet walk together, a drive in the car, or holding hands while watching television.

Companionship means you have a buddy, a best friend whom you enjoy more than any other person. You really want to spend the rest of your life with this person because you like him or her so much.

Companionship makes possible the building up of that special relationship described by the Second Vatican Council as an "intimate union of persons" that lies at the very heart of marriage. It is a kind of "super glue" that helps bond a couple for life.

Love: Love can be very difficult to define. In his First Letter to the Corinthians, Saint Paul offers a description of the kind of love necessary to keep any marriage relationship strong and healthy:

> Love is patient; love is kind; love is not envious or boastful or arrogant or rude. It does not insist on its own way; it is not irritable or resentful, it does not rejoice in wrongdoing, but rejoices in the truth. It bears all things, believes all things, hopes all things, endures all things (1 Corinthians 13:4–7).

Two individuals marrying must love each other, of course; yet, strangely enough, love is not enough. Marriage counselors routinely see couples who appear to love each other deeply but cannot live together without some degree of damage taking place. For such couples, other key components of a good relationship are not present—respect, trust, the ability to communicate deeply, or the emotional capacity to truly share their lives with each other. Love is crucial for a marriage, but it is not enough, and it is extremely important that two people contemplating marriage to each other realize and recognize this important truth.

Basic agreements: Two persons considering remarriage should be in basic agreement over such essential aspects as parenting, finances, housing, jobs and careers, sexuality, and extended family concerns. Everything needs to be talked about thoroughly prior to—not after—a marriage. Otherwise, the new marriage is crippled from the outset.

Many marriage counselors are firmly convinced that couples begin their divorce during their courtship. Negative elements creep into their relationship, and instead of eliminating them, the couple carries them right into the marriage where they prove to be deadly.

Sometimes, the very qualities that attract two people to each other ("He's so handsome and charming." "She's so beautiful.") are simply not strong enough to sustain the marriage relationship. Unfortunately, most couples realize this too late.

If you're contemplating remarriage, here are some questions to ask yourself:

- Am I still emotionally connected to my former spouse, or have I successfully separated (uncoupled) from him or her so I can go on to a new life?

- Have I successfully processed the grief, anger, and other strong emotions linked to my divorce so I will not carry some dangerous emotional baggage into a new relationship?
- Am I emotionally healthy and ready for remarriage?
- Do I feel pressured to remarry? If so, why?
- Are there "red flags" in my new relationship, things that concern me? What are they?
- How well do we communicate? Are there things my new partner and I cannot talk about? If so, why not?
- How well do we handle anger? When we get angry at each other, is it easy for us to reconcile? If not, why not?
- How well do I know myself? How well do I know my new partner?
- What are our greatest strengths and greatest weaknesses? Am I better off with or without him or her?
- Would I be remarrying for the wrong reasons, or do my reasons appear to be right?
- Is this a strong relationship, able to withstand the test of time, or are the things I find attractive in this relationship mostly superficial?
- What do I think God wants me and my new partner to do?

It is far better that a couple addresses these questions before marriage than after. In many dioceses there is now a six-month preparation time designed to help a couple prepare for marriage or remarriage following an annulment. The preparation time also provides some discernment opportunities that allow the couple to call off or postpone the marriage if they are not ready.

As in every other area of life, honesty is the best policy when it comes to addressing the multiple issues related to remarriage.

If you're not yet ready to remarry, admit that to yourself and your partner. You may be rescuing the two of you from an unhappy experience.

A key issue linked to remarriage is that of valuing yourself—an important life achievement for each of us. Valuing ourselves means we develop an inner sense about our self-worth. We no longer have to depend exclusively upon someone else telling us that we are valuable or good. We know it's true, and we believe in our own value and worth.

If you truly value yourself, it will be reflected in what you do for yourself. You will avoid behaviors and decisions that are likely to be harmful or even self-destructive. Valuing yourself must strongly color your attitudes about remarriage. It should make you look carefully for someone who will value you and whom you can value with all your heart. It should guide you in looking for a partner with whom you are truly compatible, who shares your interests and personal values. Valuing yourself leaves you far more likely to remarry out of deep desire and peace rather than out of desperation and loneliness. Valuing yourself is a manifestation of mature self-love. If two people truly value themselves and each other, it is an excellent sign for remarriage. If not, then perhaps remarriage is not yet appropriate and should be postponed.

When it comes to the issue of remarriage, the many factors discussed in this chapter need careful consideration. Whatever you do, don't rush the discernment/decision process. Give yourself all the time you need, draw upon every resource available to you, and listen closely to what God has to say as you try to make your decision about this all-important life event.

Conclusion

Shannon has been divorced for a year. "Exactly one year, two weeks, and five days," she insists. "A divorce is such a major life event that I guess you never forget—much the same way you never forget your wedding day."

When asked what the past year has been like, Shannon pauses thoughtfully. "Tough. To be honest, it was pure hell at times. But you know what? I'm still here, and I'm now starting to see light at the end of the tunnel." She waves her hand through the air. "No! More than that. I believe the tunnel is now behind me!"

What helped Shannon through the past year?

"Many, many things, especially my faith in God. And, oh, yes, one other important thing comes to mind. Early on, when I realized we really would get divorced, I decided to view myself as a survivor and not a victim.

"I decided that my divorce would not become my tombstone but a steppingstone to a new and better life. I held on tenaciously to that conviction and gradually began to make the choices and decisions that have brought me to this point." She smiles. "I'm happy to say that this is a pretty good point to be at. I'm doing just fine now."

Shannon's brief statement is a testimony to the fact that healing can and does take place following the trauma of divorce. The failure of a marriage need not be fatal. Nor does divorce have to unleash some terrible dark curse that leaves you sad and mad for a lifetime.

This book has looked at divorce through the lens of healing. It has been our contention that divorce generally requires some degree of emotional and spiritual healing, and we've highlighted a number of ways in which the healing process can be approached.

We urge you to make your own personal healing a major priority following your divorce. Give yourself all the care, compassion, understanding, attention, and time you deserve.

Especially time! Healing cannot be hurried. It tends to manifest itself gradually and quietly until one day you're aware that it's taken place, and you feel whole again.

Remember that God is always with you to guide and direct you, to touch you with healing love, and to remind you that you can never be a failure because you are a precious daughter or son. Take God's hand and walk courageously into your future. May you come to know that with the help of God's grace, all things—yes, even your divorce—can work together for good. As your faith and trust in God deepen, may you discover this great truth for yourself.

Appendix 1

Using the Internet Wisely and Well

Todd found the early morning hours the hardest of all to bear. After switching channels on the TV, he found himself drawn to his computer. His Internet service provider (ISP) offered a variety of free services including instant messaging, chat rooms, personals, and a search engine. He began surfing for his hobbies—golf and fishing. While online, he began to get little messages that would pop up on his screen. At first, not knowing what they were, he just ignored them. Then, he began to see the same names popping up when he would log in. Some were pretty funny, and he replied to them. And then the tone became more adult. The pop-ups grew in number and were pornographic in nature. He became curious, visited the free sites. Soon Todd was online most of the night, in a virtual world where every wish was granted. His work suffered, he was isolated from his friends. He had become addicted.

Marianne would find the time after the kids went to bed heavy on her hands. Sitting with them while doing their homework on the Internet, she began to enjoy the new worlds it opened up to her. Reading was a passion, and she enjoyed the author chats that took place on Saturday mornings. She enjoyed the news services and considered herself pretty savvy.

During an online chat with her book club members, she had an instant message saying "hello." Assuming it was one of the group, she responded and had a good conversation. Two nights later she received an e-mail from the person who had sent her the instant message, saying he was coming to her area, and maybe they could do coffee at the local bookstore. She declined.

A few days later an actual letter arrived, signed by the e-mail sender. Marianne was startled. How had they found her? One afternoon she heard her daughter speaking to someone on the phone: "My mom's name is Marianne, let me get her for you. No, my dad doesn't live here anymore." Marianne's heart stopped. It was the person from the e-mail. She took the phone, told him she had caller ID, and was reporting him to the authorities. For months she was worried that he would show up. Her friends said they had had similar invasions. They told her to look at her Internet profile. Sure enough, what she mistook for a registration form for her e-mail provider was online for other members to see—first and last names, address, phones and hobbies. "How stupid could I have been?!"

There are a number of resources on the Internet and in every library that you may find helpful.

Searching the Internet

It isn't just children who are vulnerable on the Internet. Innocent or inexperienced adult users may find themselves targets of con artists instead of recipients of good information. For those who know their way around in search engines, there are a great number of informational sites. For those who do not, there are places and people waiting to prey on the lonely, the lost, and the inexperienced. Be the adult, and do your homework.

How Do I Recognize Safe Internet Sites?

Knowing the author of the sites is critical. Some safe sites are those recognized by the U.S. Catholic Church. The address or "url" should be easily recognized without a lot symbols and strange characters. If you don't recognize the name or the extension, stay away. (Generally non-profit and religious sites will end with ".org" for "organization." However, they may use .com "commercial" or .net "network" as well. Government sites will end in ".gov" and colleges in ".edu.")

Site addresses change often, so what brought up good information for "Catholic Singles" yesterday, may be pornography sites today. A few years ago, a number of Catholic dioceses let their domain names (Internet addresses) expire, and they were taken over by pornography sites, who posed in search engines (Internet catalogs) as the former diocesan site.

Some good sites are listed in Appendix 2. You may wish to begin with *www.USCCB.org*, or your (arch)diocesan or parish Web sites. National Catholic publishing houses, for example, *www.liguori.org*, will give you access to reputable printed resources.

E-mail names and **profiles** are how you are known on the Internet. It is a common mistake to use professional and home e-mail addresses when you register for information or to participate in chat rooms or discussion groups. Like Marianne, too often adults fill out personal information in their profile including actual names, addresses, home and work phones. Create a "junk e-mail" to register to participate in these forums. You will avoid spam (junk mail), viruses, and much more. Only give your personal and work emails to family and friends, just as you would your real mailing address and phone numbers. **Never**

give out your passwords or personal information to the public, watch for secure sites (symbol is a locked padlock), and know your vendors.

Chat Rooms are not good ideas for beginners. Even those that are considered "town hall" groups rated "G" are often stalked by professionals who are trying to send instant messages as pop-ups. Check their profile, and don't respond if you don't know who they are.

Appendix 2

Suggestions for Reliable Resources

In the following list of resources, words within the brackets are search-engine friendly words.

Education

(Under "State Employment Commissions" include)
- Displaced Homemaker Programs (employment and training programs) [displaced homemaker]
- Workforce Investment Act Adult Program [workforce act]

Job Placement/Career Guidance

Having access to a computer can make job searching much easier. Every library offers free Internet connections and computer savvy librarians to assist you.

There are many Web sites that offer career and guidance counseling. Many offer free introductory samples. [career] [jobs] Some good sites, at time of publishing: *www.monster.com*; *www.assessment.com*; *www.jobs.com*.

USA Jobs, the federal government's official job site, *www.usajobs .opm.gov*. Also offers free résumé options [government jobs] [federal jobs] [state jobs] [state employment] also *www.usps.com* for US Postal Service listings.

Résumé writing: [résumé] Also check your word-processing program's templates for résumé writer "wizards" to walk you through style and content suggestions.

Housing Assistance

The Housing Rights Committee is an affiliate of the National Alliance of HUD-Tenants, a member of the National Low-Income Housing Coalition, *www.hrcsf.org* [federal subsidized housing] *www.hud.gov* [FHA housing].

Personal Guidance

OnceCatholic—a pastoral outreach on the Internet by the Franciscan Friars of St. John the Baptist Province, Cincinnati, Ohio, *www.OnceCatholic.org* combines Catholic counselors with online town-hall meetings for people who are facing challenges to their Catholicity. Particularly helpful is the room, "Marriage Issues."

Parish Nurse Program, International Parish Nurse Resource Center (IPNRC), *www.parishnurses.org* [Catholic parish nurses]—many parishes offer these trained health professionals as part of their outreach to the local Catholic community: 475 East Lockwood Avenue, St. Louis, MO 63119; (314) 918-2559, Fax: (314) 918-2558.

Self-Help Groups

North American Conference of Separated and Divorced Catholics (NACSDC), founded 1975, a network of support for families experiencing separation and divorce. NACSDC Central Office, P.O. Box 360, Richland, OR 97870; phone: (541) 893-6089; fax: (541) 893-6089 *51; *www.nacsdc.org*; e-mail: *info@nacsdc.org*.

Beginning Experience—founded 1974, based on the premise of Marriage Encounter, BE was designed as a spiritual journey weekend and journey for separated, divorced, and widowed individuals. *www.beginningexperience.org*, Beginning Experience International Ministry Center, 1657 Commerce Drive, Suite 2B, South Bend, IN 46628; (574) 283-0279, or toll free 866-610-8877 (US and Canada); fax (574) 283-0287.

Internet Groups

As we mentioned before, use caution when joining forums, chats, personal ads, and dating services. **Do not give out personal information and home phone numbers.** When considering a Catholic singles or divorced group, find out what dioceses they are located in. Call that diocese. Are they recognized by the bishop? Do they have trained Catholic counselors? What are their fees? What are the prerequisites to calling themselves "Catholic"? Ask for references you can check out. If your diocese or pastor doesn't recognize them, then stay away.

At time of printing some reputable Catholic singles groups: *www.avemariasingles.com;www.straphael.net; www.catholicsingles.com* and your own diocese may offer special ministry for widowed, single, and divorced Catholics.